"Dr. Debilal Mishra's 'Understanding Happiness' is a beacon of hope in today's fast-paced world, illuminating the path to a fulfilling life. By delving into the psychological underpinnings of happiness, this book empowers readers with a profound understanding of what truly matters. As emotional turmoil and professional pressures mount, 'Understanding Happiness' offers a timely intervention, inspiring readers to pause, reflect, and rediscover their purpose."

Dr Chittaranjan Nayak
Professor of Economics
North Eastern Hill University, Shillong

"Since happiness is a much sought-after phenomenon in recent times, Dr Debilal Mishra's 'Understanding Happiness' appears to be rewarding as well as worthwhile. With an empirically emphatic undertone the book occasions a quintessence of positive motivation towards life. In a perennial world of emotional complexities leading to professional challenges, the work assures some hope to reflect, restart and move forward."

Nilambar Rath
Founder Editor & CEO, OdishaLIVE Media Network;
Formerly, Editor, ETV & News18 (Odia),
Network 18 Group;
Communication expert, trainer & educator

From the best-selling author of Communication, a Poetic Approach

Understanding Happiness
A Self-motivational approach to Self-management
Debilal Mishra

With a Foreword by
Prof. Sangeeta Rath

BLACK EAGLE BOOKS
Dublin, USA | Bhubaneswar, India

Black Eagle Books
USA address:
7464 Wisdom Lane
Dublin, OH 43016

E-mail: info@blackeaglebooks.org
Website: www.blackeaglebooks.org

First International Edition Published by
Black Eagle Books, 2025

UNDERSTANDING HAPPINESS
by **Debilal Mishra**

Copyright © Debilal Mishra

All rights reserved. No part of this publication may be reproduced, stored in a retrieval system, or transmitted, in any form or by any means, electronic, mechanical, photocopying, recording or otherwise without the prior permission of the publisher.

Cover & Interior Design: Ezy's Publication

ISBN- 978-1-64560-724-3 (Paperback)

Printed in the United States of America

Happiness

Happiness lies within
It can't be found without
You may invest everything,
But in the end
Only you can make yourself happy;
You can't buy it
You can't sell it
It's something you can only feel and realize
Once you become one with the deeper self,
Beyond any shape or size;

Happiness is a choice,
And is always in the offing,
If you can connect to yourself from within,
The signals of happiness will never go missing!

-The Author

FOREWORD

In a world where the pursuit of happiness often feels elusive and external circumstances dictate our emotional state, Dr Debilal Mishra's *Understanding Happiness: A Self-Motivational Approach to Self-Management* arrives as a beacon of clarity and empowerment. This book is not merely a collection of ideas—it is a carefully crafted guide that invites readers to embark on a transformative journey toward self-awareness, resilience, and authentic joy. Dr Mishra's insightful approach challenges conventional thinking by emphasizing that happiness is not a destination granted by others or by fate, but a conscious, self-motivated choice anchored in personal management and inner strength. Drawing on a rich tapestry of wisdom, practical strategies, and profound reflections, this work equips readers with the tools to navigate life's challenges while fostering a sustainable sense of well-being.

What sets this book apart is its unique fusion of motivation and self-management, offering readers a blueprint to cultivate a mindset that is both positive and proactive. It encourages us to take responsibility for our emotional landscape, teaching us how to harness our thoughts, habits, and actions to create a life that resonates with purpose and contentment. *Understanding Happiness* is a timely and essential read for anyone seeking to reclaim control over their mental and emotional health. Whether you are struggling with everyday stress, grappling with deeper existential questions, or simply striving to live more fully, Dr Mishra's work provides not only inspiration but also actionable wisdom.

In a world often shadowed by doubt, competition, and uncertainty, the greatest act of courage is to nurture a positive and resilient mind. This collection of articles is a journey — not through abstract philosophy, but through lived wisdom, emotional clarity, and thoughtful insight into what it truly means to live with purpose and perspective.

Each chapter of this book explores a vital aspect of personal growth. From the profound power of a positive mindset that unlocks hidden possibilities, to the quiet strength of optimism that reorients our gaze toward hope, the insights within these pages are both timely and timeless.

We examine the complex dance between failure and success, not as opposites, but as partners in growth. These reflections guide readers to understand that success is not a destination, but a process — one that is informed by courage, reflection, and the willingness to rise, again and again. In recognizing our unique talents, we are reminded that the most authentic communication flows not from imitation, but from self-awareness. Whether in our personal or professional lives, honoring our individuality allows us to express ourselves with conviction and clarity. Reflecting on experiences and embracing change are presented as strategies to lead a meaningful life. We can harness technology to enhance our lives without compromising our emotional health and human values.

Finally, in confronting the quiet battles of the soul — depression, self-doubt, and the need for self-acceptance — these articles offer not judgment, but empathy. They call on readers to embrace themselves with the same compassion they extend to others, and to believe that healing begins with acknowledgment and love.

This book is not just a guide; it's a companion for anyone seeking a more conscious, intentional, and empowered life. Whether you are at the beginning of your personal journey or already walking the path of self-discovery, these words will resonate, uplift, and reaffirm your inner strength. As you turn these pages, prepare to be inspired, challenged, and ultimately transformed. This is more than a book; it is an invitation to cultivate happiness from within, to become your own greatest source of motivation, and to master the art of self-management for a richer, more fulfilling life.

Let these reflections inspire you to think more deeply, live more fully, and above all, believe in the extraordinary power of your own mind.

Prof. (Dr) Sangeeta Rath
Formerly, Professor and Head, Dept of Psychology, Utkal University and Ravenshaw University; Adjunct Professor, Indian Institute of Technology, Bhubaneswar; and Member, Odisha Public Service Commission.

CONTENTS

Failure and Success	13
Adjustment	16
Self-belief	19
Positive Vibes	22
Misunderstanding	25
Positive Life	28
Nature of a Teacher	32
Patience	36
Mental Health	39
Staying Calm	43
The Power of our Habits	46
Technology and Peace	50
People and Natures	54
Positive Leadership	57
Relationship	61
Depression	65
Finding Happiness	68
Stress, Fitness & Positive Personality	72
Ego and Life	79
Digital Communication and Human Relationship	82
Self-management and motivation	86
Importance of Mother Language	90
Public Relations	94

FAILURE AND SUCCESS

What is failure?
Failure is just a state of mind, nothing else! It originates in the absence of efforts. As long as we keep trying with no loss of spirit, no failure can ever occur. It all depends on how we think. Our thoughts can either make us or break us. In every circumstance we must learn to think great. Every experience in life is meaningful and counts in the long run. We learn from what we do! Not being able to achieve a particular goal can't be seen as a failure; since we keep learning in the process and can use that experience for even bigger purposes.

What does it take to overcome the feeling of failure?
It takes positivity, passion, patience and perseverance. We must understand that as long as we keep loving and believing in ourselves, nothing can ever stop our progress. There can be no failure once we start to feel ourselves, our efforts; and when there can be no failure, we don't have to worry!

Why are people often driven into a state of failure despite being aware of things?
Basically, this happens for two reasons. First, they have some unrelated or ungrounded imagination about success. Second, they focus more on the goal, rather than the efforts it takes. We can put in efforts. That's all we can do. Our

efforts may lead to something, either we have desired, or we haven't desired. If we get the desired result we succeed—that's how we perceive success and failure after all. But this, under no circumstances, is a healthy calculation. We must focus on the sincerity of the efforts all the time. Our efforts often create our true identity and character we may have never imagined! We must remember that goal may change, but the glory stays forever; and for achieving this glory we need to focus on the efforts determinedly without thinking much about the smaller things around.

How can one be successful in the real sense of the term?

The first thing we need is an unflinching faith in ourselves. Believing is achieving indeed! Our every effort should be replete with our ever-growing inner strength. There should be no fear, no doubt, and no confusion. We should be clear to ourselves. Competency results from conviction. Success largely depends on our will to continue even when we can't! A tremendous will, constant love and perseverance will make it for sure! There must be no comparison with anyone since we all are naturally unique. Success is all about the self-exploration for a larger purpose and in the greater interest of our true growth. The real success lies in our inner happiness. Observed minutely, success is a matter of effort; effort is a matter of commitment; and commitment is a matter of conviction. Exploration leads to excellence. All our strengths are waiting to be explored; and the more we explore, the more we excel!

Mind what matters!!!

- As long as we keep trying with no loss of spirit, no failure can ever occur.
- Every experience in life is meaningful and counts in the long run.
- As long as we keep loving and believing in ourselves, nothing can ever stop our progress!
- Our efforts often create our true identity and character we may have never imagined!
- The first thing we need is an unflinching faith in ourselves.
- Success largely depends on our will to continue even when we can't!
- There must be no comparison with anyone since we all are naturally unique.
- Success is a matter of effort; effort is a matter of commitment; and commitment is a matter of conviction.

ADJUSTMENT

Why is adjustment important in life?

In our lives there are many situations where we may not like certain things, but we certainly can't live without them. This is where we need to adjust. Adjustment is a psychological phenomenon and a behavioral process. We are living in an environment that is dynamic both physically and emotionally. Everything is changing every moment. So, we must be in a position to adjust to the changing conditions; otherwise, we may fall short of our desired destination! That's why adjustment is central to success in various contexts.

What are the important qualities needed for adjustment?

We need to remember that there can be no adjustment without acceptance. Acceptance creates the much needed space for adjustment. If we can't accept a situation, we will keep on resisting. And as long as we keep on resisting, we can hardly adjust to it. So, the will to change and accept is quite paramount and of capital significance as far as the question of adjustment is concerned.

What are the major challenges to acceptance?

The major challenge is one's ego. If there is ego, the scope for acceptance is scantier. Ego never lets us accept things it doesn't like; but, when the situation is that important, we need to manage the ego accordingly. Another challenge is our intransigent ever-the-same attitude. We need to change our attitude as per the demands of the situation. Without adequate attitudinal and behavioral changes, it is really hard to accept people and the situations around. Change becomes a challenge for those who lack the ability to adjust.

How to move forward without something we like?

Happiness is certainly a state of mind. We need to manage our mind in the best possible manner. We can't get what we want always. Life is a journey of ups and downs. Nothing is just the same for a long time. We need to adjust constantly and move forward. The process of self-exploration and self-motivation is all so vital. Moreover, one must reflect on every experience and realize the realities involved therein; since experience is the root of life's wisdom. It's only by creating newer spaces for newer things within that we can lead a meaningful life that mostly consists in learning, realization, change and adjustment.

Mind what matters!!!

- Adjustment is central to success in various contexts
- Acceptance creates the much needed space for adjustment.
- Ego never lets us accept things it doesn't like.
- Without adequate attitudinal and behavioral changes, it is really hard to accept people and the situations around.
- Happiness is certainly a state of mind.
- Change becomes a challenge for those who lack the ability to adjust.

SELF-BELIEF

How can one get hold of the self-belief?
Everyone in this world is unique. That way, everyone is having certain unique capability. We may not be equally talented, but we are uniquely talented. We need to be sure about the fact that there's some unique capability in us that makes us outstandingly different from others. Believing is achieving. There can be no conquest without conviction. We need to realize and explore our potentially divine strengths we are born with. Swami Vivekananda once said, "In order to succeed one must have tremendous perseverance and tremendous will". In every challenging and adverse situation our real self gets unfolded! All we need are purpose, passion, patience and perseverance!

There are situations that break us. In this context, how can we start believing in ourselves?
If there are no hard times, there can be no good times. Every situation has something positive for us. If we can learn the right lesson at the right time, we can definitely become the better versions of ourselves. Life is a university in itself. Learning from every experience and moving forward with the positive learning is what it keeps teaching! We are certainly affected by what we learn. Learning positive things would definitely strengthen us; and learning negative things would weaken us from

all sides. There is always a chance to prove our unique capability. It's never too late to be there. With determined efforts, patience and an unflinching faith we can make our own destiny, no matter what we may be undergoing!

What if we have no one with us in the journey?

Everyone's journey in life is unique and so is their destination. Why should we expect someone to be with us all the while? We must learn to be with ourselves. It always takes some toil to unwrap the box that carries a precious gift. If we can't struggle, or if we shy away from the tough times, we can hardly unpack and unleash the ever wonderful person in us. We should never be afraid of the journey if we are alone; rather, we should keep enjoying every step, every turn and every twist! That alone will make it beautiful. We should remember that we are never defeated, as long as we have the will to win.

How to build ourselves as better persons?

According to Swami Vivekananda, "all power is within you. You can do anything and everything." We must believe in that power within. Our belief must lead us to persevere; and nothing is impossible for a persevering mind. The more we can believe, the better we can prepare; and a better preparation always leads to a better performance. Life is a process of learning, exploring and becoming the best versions of ourselves. As Sri Aurobindo has put it, "Arise, transcend Thyself, Thou art man and the whole nature of man is to become more than himself." We should understand that the storm may come, and the storm may go; but, the tree, that is still there, brings undying hopes to many!

Mind what matters!!!

- Everyone in this world is unique.
- There can be no conquest without conviction. Every situation has something positive for us.
- We are certainly affected by what we learn.
- Everyone's journey in life is unique and so is their destination.
- We are never defeated, as long as we have the will to win.
- Our belief determines our preparation; our preparation determines our performance.
- Life is a process of learning, exploring and becoming the best versions of ourselves.

POSITIVE VIBES

How can positive vibes be created?

Positive vibes can be created by positive thoughts; and for that we need to make the mind positive. A positive mind is the source of the positive energy. When the mind is positive, there's a positive behavioral transformation leading to a positive life. Without a positive mind, a positive life is simply inconceivable.

How can we make the mind positive?

Self-realization is really crucial in this process. A positive mind is certainly the result of positive learning, realization and positive relationships. A positive mind realizes its unique capability; and it never compares, competes or expects. It consists in the attitude to see and explore possibilities in everything.

How can one create a positive personality?

It's only by loving and believing in oneself that one can create a positive personality. Whatever may be the situation, one must choose effort over excuses; resilience over regrets; work over weaknesses; learning over losses; and goals over gaps. Self-belief and self-love are two vital components. Love for ourselves strengthens our self-belief and creates an aura and atmosphere of positive vibes.

How can we protect our positivity in negative situations?

We must have faith in our positivity and keep away from negative vibes as much as possible. We should stop taking something or someone seriously if they negatively affect us. There should be selective responses. 'Respond to what matters the most!' We should not overburden the mind with the pressure to react to everything. Gratuitous reactions often result in loss of mental peace. Moreover, we need to develop positive interests as central to our positive habits and emotions. Being with positive energy is always crucial. We need to explore such sources around: be it books, stories, events, activities, people or places!

We should focus more on 'what we have', 'what we learn' and 'what we can do', instead of getting too much concerned about 'what we don't have', and 'what we can't do'. We must remember that a positive mind always finds a reason to be positive, whereas a negative mind always finds a reason to be negative. Locking the negative mind through persistent practice, and unlocking the positive mind through love, belief and learning is central to all our endeavours for excellence.

Mind what matters!!!

- Positive vibes can be created by positive thoughts.
- A positive mind never compares, competes or expects.
- It's only by loving and believing in oneself that one can create a positive personality.
- There should be selective responses—respond to what matters the most!
- A positive mind always finds a reason to be positive, whereas a negative mind always finds a reason to be negative.
- The positive mind can be unlocked through love, belief and learning.

MISUNDERSTANDING

How does misunderstanding occur in our lives?

It occurs due to several reasons including but not limited to our ego-centric nature, lack of trust and sensitivity, and, of course, ignorance. Sometimes, we are so self-driven, that we hardly have a heart for others. We always think we are right. We may be right, but being right doesn't essentially mean being insensitive or unconcerned. To understand someone is never easy. It involves a psychic process replete with sensitivity, receptivity and connectivity based on patience and trust. Lack of trust is always central to misunderstanding.

How does misunderstanding affect our lives?

It can create some worst disasters. Lack of understanding often leads to the crises of various natures affecting every part of our lives. Simply put, 'No understanding' means 'No trust'; 'No trust' means 'No acceptance'; and 'No acceptance' means 'No relationship'. Life is affected this way.

How can we remove misunderstanding?

We need to bring some changes to our nature—the ways we think and react. We can remove misunderstanding only by understanding. There's no other satisfying way. In our lives, sometimes, we can't understand;

sometimes, we don't want to understand; and sometimes, we misunderstand. When we can't understand, it's our ignorance; when we don't want to understand, it's our ego; and when we misunderstand, it's lack of trust. We need to manage ourselves accordingly.

Communication plays a major role in our relationships. The nature of our communication influences the nature of our relationship; and the nature of our relationship also influences the nature of our communication. That way, we must understand to communicate and communicate to understand. Understanding someone consists in understanding the situation they are in. We usually have a tendency to view the communication without viewing its underlying situation which is more important. In order to avoid misunderstanding, we must have control over our reactions and understand the situation in its entirety. It's a matter of communicating with purpose, knowledge and connectivity ultimately.

What is ideal communication in the context of a relationship?

Ideal communication is based on sensitivity, understanding, good intentions, and, above all, love. Understanding the message and the receiver is of capital importance. Our communication should result from and result in understanding. In a sense, the sender needs to encode according to the decoding capacity of the receiver. The sender's message is meaningless if the receiver fails to understand it. We need to mind our intentions as well. Good intention and trust go together. Our communication should carry both. Then only can it be ideal!

Mind what matters!!!

- To understand someone is never easy. It takes sensitivity, receptivity and connectivity based on patience and trust.
- 'No understanding' means 'No trust'; 'No trust' means 'No acceptance'; and 'No acceptance' means 'No relationship'.
- We can remove misunderstanding only by understanding.
- When we can't understand, it's our ignorance; when we don't want to understand, it's our ego; and when we misunderstand, it's lack of trust.
- The nature of our communication influences the nature of our relationship and vice-versa.
- Understanding someone consists more in understanding the situation they are in.
- Ideal communication is based on sensitivity, understanding, good intentions, and, above all, love.
- Our communication should result from and result in understanding.

POSITIVE LIFE

How can one stay positive in every situation?
Staying positive is not that tough. First of all, we need to love and believe in ourselves. We can if we think we can with a sense of conviction and commitment. The nature of our thoughts ultimately determines the nature of our lives. Most of the times, we think a lot, and are worried, anxious and tense over certain things. That doesn't help at all. There are always two crucial options in life—let's change it if we can or let's accept it and work on our strengths with a greater degree of faith. So, there is practically no place for stress or worry at all.

How can one stay away from worries of the everyday life?
It's very simple. If we can, why worry? If we can't, why worry? We need to understand that negative thoughts never help us achieve our goals; and they also never solve our hard-hitting problems. At the end of the day, we have to deal with it. So, if we have to deal with it anyway, then why shouldn't we face it with positivity, hope and right spirit? If we'll be positive in any situation, the effort will be more effective and it will lead us closer to the goal or some solution. Negativity never works for anyone! Whatever may be the situation, we must not lose our sense of conviction, commitment and the spirit to make headway.

How can one find hope amidst negativity?

We should remember that a positive mind always finds a reason to be positive, whereas a negative mind always finds a reason to be negative. We have both the minds within. We must block the negative mind forever the way we block some people or pages we don't like on the various social media platforms. It isn't at all impossible. In fact, nothing is impossible for a calm, passionate and persevering mind. We may choose a goal and we mayn't be able to achieve that; but, here the positive mind will explore the experience, learning and the true progress that we have made. It will keep focusing on the sincerity of the efforts that never goes in vain. Success and failure are but the different states of the mind. It is how we look at something that determines our outlook and it affects our life in a big way.

One shouldn't fear failure. Right?

There is no failure absolutely. Life is a process of learning and moving forward. It's more about effort and progress. We should be having a positive attitude in every situation. Celebration of every moment is the essence of life. We must explore our inner beauty and let our unique capability define ourselves. Life may give us tough situations, but we can increase our inner space and capacity! We mayn't control the circumstances, but we can control ourselves evermore! If we can unfailingly get hold of ourselves, life will definitely be a joyous thing!

How to deal with the negative vibes around?

Everyone is having their own nature. We behave the way we think. We shouldn't feel disturbed by anyone's behaviour since their perceptions about ourselves are not always correct. It's more like "I perceive you the way you impress me," but, the truth or reality lies beyond the compass of impression and perception. You alone know who you are. None else can! So, we shouldn't lose our positivity due to someone's negative nature. Let them be there! Our positivity is enough! We mustn't perceive ourselves in accordance with the perception of someone else. It's never wise to lose our own positivity for someone's negativity. That's a very bad deal! Whatever may be the situation, we should never stop loving and believing in ourselves. Let's bring in some more positive vibes, if there are some negative vibes around! We always have the scope to disconnect from the negativity and connect to the positivity surrounding us; and it takes some conscious and committed efforts in the process.

Mind what matters!!!

- The nature of our thoughts ultimately determines the nature of our lives.
- Whatever may be the situation, we must not lose our sense of conviction, commitment and the spirit to make headway.
- Success and failure are but the different states of the mind. It is how we look at something that determines our outlook and it affects our life in a big way.
- "I perceive you the way you impress me".
- We mustn't perceive ourselves in accordance with the perception of someone else.
- It's never wise to lose our own positivity for someone's negativity.

NATURE OF A TEACHER

What are the common challenges before the teachers in the present time?

A teacher's job is always challenging. There are basically three sets of challenges before a teacher: behavioural, infrastructural and ideological. The behavioural challenges comprise the dynamics of the relationship with the students, colleagues and authorities. There are situations in which the mental, emotional and moral strengths of a teacher are tested. If a teacher is not having behavioural stability, he or she can neither exert a desirable influence on the students; nor can they create an atmosphere conducive to effective learning and motivation. Infrastructural challenges have to do with working equipment, access to technology, technological competency, available scopes for exposure and meaningful activities. Ideological challenges basically result from the gap between what the teachers believe and what they feel in various contexts. Unwanted external and internal factors together pose stronger ideological challenges before a teacher.

How can a teacher overcome these challenges?

A teacher needs to learn constantly. They need to improve upon themselves every moment by way of purpose, passion, patience and perseverance. We need to remember that being a teacher is not everyone's cup of tea. It takes a great degree of self-control, self-exploration, self-belief and self-motivation. Therefore, the teachers need to work on their mental skills that involve managing emotions, ego and temperament as central to a better self-management. Simply put, it takes a lot of character to be a teacher.

How can an ideal teacher character be created?

Usually, there are two types of teachers: teachers by choice and teachers by chance. Those who are teachers by choice can make greater sacrifices as far as the goals are concerned; whereas those who are teachers by chance are concerned about narrow interests centred on personal comforts and benefits. The former believes in the achievements of the students and the larger social good, and the latter grows with qualities common to any profession.

A teacher's character is built on love, empathy, conviction, realization, effort, values and a greater degree of self-control. According to Swami Vivekananda, 'the teacher must not only possess the knowledge he is to transmit to the student, but he must also know how to transmit it. The only true teacher is he who can immediately come down to the level of the student, and transfer his soul to the student's soul and see through the student's eyes and hear through His ears and understand through his mind. Such a teacher can really teach and none else can.'

Who is a great teacher?

A great teacher understands and inspires! More importantly, they love the efforts replete with learning and connectivity. The students love a teacher only when they find in them a great source of motivation. A teacher must strive to be a role model for the students. In the words of Scott Hayden, 'teachers have three loves: love of learning, love of learners, and the love of bringing the first two loves together.' A teacher needs to create a greater influence on the strength of an inspiring personality. That way, a teacher can make a difference in someone's life. Just as Sidney Hook has put it, 'everyone who remembers his own education remembers teachers, not methods and techniques. The teacher is the heart of the educational system.'

Mind what matters!!!

- Being a teacher is not everyone's cup of tea. It takes a great degree of self-control, self-exploration, self-belief and self-motivation.
- A great teacher understands and inspires!
- A teacher needs to learn constantly.
- The teachers need to work on their mental skills that involve managing emotions, ego and temperament as central to a better self-management.

PATIENCE

Why patience is important in life?

Without patience, we can never move forward. Patience is central to perseverance. In life, we face so many situations, and every situation is unique. Patience helps us stand strong, learn from the situations and hope for the best. According to Swami Vivekananda, purity, patience and perseverance are the three essentials to success. A truly successful life is undoubtedly and inevitably built on the virtues of patience.

How can one have patience when there is so much of turmoil around?

Patience is all about behaving with inner strengths, hope and wisdom. The inner strengths create a steadfast character to face and learn from any situation. Learning from the experiences results in wisdom. One needs to grow wise with the experiences. Patience is possible only when one believes in their inner strengths and wisdom. Therefore, self-belief is the key to being patient in every situation.

What are the fundamental challenges to patience?

Yes, there can be various challenges including but not limited to ego, ignorance, expectations and weaknesses. Patience calls for effective self-control and management. Being patient is not being weak; rather, it is being balanced. Without patience we can neither face a stronger situation nor can we learn from it. Patience makes us persevere with no loss of faith and flow.

How can we be patient in all situations?

It's by understanding a situation and believing in our strengths that we can be patient. According to Carl Jung, a great Psychologist, 'Even a happy life cannot be without a measure of darkness, and the word happy would lose its meaning if it were not balanced by sadness. It is far better to take things as they come along with patience and equanimity.' Patience mostly consists in one's ability to be calm in a situation that is quite disturbing; and for this one has to be positively spacious from within. A patient mind learns to accept things and convert them into opportunities for greater growth.

How are patience and happiness related to each other?

When someone is impatient, they lose their inner balance. The loss of inner balance leads to the loss of inner peace which, in turn, ensures the loss of happiness. Impatience leads to behavioural instability, whereas patience causes stability and progress. If you are patient, you can control your emotions and manage them effectively. An impatient mind is always vulnerable to situations. Patience in life signifies personality made up of purity of strength and positivity.

Mind what matters!!!

- A truly successful life is undoubtedly and inevitably built on the virtues of patience.
- Patience is all about behaving with inner strengths, hope and wisdom.
- There can be no patience without self-belief.
- Patience calls for effective self-control and management. Being patient is not being weak; rather, it's being balanced.
- Patience makes us persevere with no loss of faith and flow.
- A patient mind learns to accept things and convert them into opportunities for greater growth.
- When someone is impatient, they lose their inner balance.

MENTAL HEALTH

How can we understand mental health?

The mental health primarily concerns our ability to think, feel, and act as desired by the situation we are in. The concept of mental health involves our psychological, emotional and behavioural well-being. Our mental health plays a crucial role in determining our overall growth and progress.

What are the major challenges to the mental health?

Negative environment is one of such major challenges. Human mind is a complex phenomenon. Moreover, it's largely susceptible to the emotional dynamics of our environment. That way, positive thoughts have a positive bearing on the mind and the negative thoughts have a negative bearing. Emotional factors like hatred, loneliness, excessive expectation, immoderate dependency, sense of failure, hopelessness, psychological alienation, inordinate attachment to something/someone etc exercise a negative control on our minds and it all affects our sense of being.

How can the mental health be protected?

Our mental health is our own responsibility. It can't be left to anyone else. A good mental health thrives on two important conditions: self-love and self-belief. As long as we keep loving and believing in ourselves, no situation can ever affect our composure. We need to understand that everyone in this world is unique, and so are their psychological ways of response and behavior. We simply can't expect everyone to behave the way we like. We mustn't believe that we are weak or mentally impoverished. Effort creates hope. We need to focus on that. We need to have self-awareness and practice healthy detachment in the context of emotional dependency and expectations. The real happiness lies within. Self-exploration adds meaning to our life.

More importantly, whenever we have a relationship we must respect it. Lack of respect signifies lack of love; and lack of love is always detrimental to our mental health. We must listen to people around us. It takes patience and understanding. We mayn't be able to do anything at times, but we can show a sensitive heart. That can do a lot! Positive communication certainly acts as a medicine. It can help restore the emotional balance. Sometimes, we don't have the idea that when we start communicating we start solving various unseen and unsaid problems!

What should someone do when they face such challenging situations?

Instead of fearing, we must start working on the solution of every problem. An unflinching faith in our inner strengths is central to all our endeavours for excellence. We need to keep in mind that emotions lead to attachment and attachment leads to expectations. Our mental state is somewhere prone to our expectations. Emotions bring positive experiences as long as we can manage them. If uncontrolled, the emotions may lead to a lot of trouble. We need to lock the negative mind that often expects, competes and compares; and we must unlock and unleash the positive mind that believes, explores and celebrates. We must keep immune to all negativity, negative vibes.

Talk to people you like. Even if there is no one, spend some time with yourself and see how wonderful you are! Do what gives you some positive energy. Have some positive vibes around you. Follow your creative passion. Express the real yourself and, more importantly, stay fearless. There can be no beautiful life without a beautiful mind; and it's only by our inner positivity and creativity that we can achieve a beautiful mind. Moreover, life can be more beautiful if we can replace fear with faith, pain with patience, loathing with love, despair with dreams, and ego with enlightenment!

Mind what matters!!!

- Our mental health plays a crucial role in determining our overall growth and progress.
- Positive thoughts have a positive bearing on the mind and the negative thoughts have a negative bearing.
- Our mental health is our own responsibility. It can't be left to anyone else.
- As long as we keep loving and believing in ourselves, no situation can ever affect our composure.
- The real happiness lies within. Self-exploration adds meaning to our life.
- We must unlock and unleash the positive mind that believes, explores and celebrates.
- There can be no beautiful life without a beautiful mind; and it's only by our inner positivity and creativity that we can achieve a beautiful mind.
- Life can be more beautiful if we can replace fear with faith, pain with patience, loathing with love, despair with dreams and ego with enlightenment!

STAYING CALM

How does calmness help us?

First of all, there's is a great energy and focus in being calm. Inner calmness helps in self-exploration and facilitates self-awareness. When we are calm we can concentrate more on the ideas we are after. Moreover, calmness is an essential ingredient of creativity and concentration. Not only does it sustain the creative energies, but it also helps them thrive to the greatest possible degree.

How can one be calm in turbulent situations?

Whatever may be the situation, one can still be calm! In fact, staying calm from within helps us in handling the situation in a better way. Taking stress or getting tense never solves a problem; rather, it worsens the situation further. We must realize that one's best self functions only when there's calmness inside. To be calm one has to explore the inner depth, trust, and sense of acceptance. The more vast you are from within, the lesser perturbed you are. It's the calmness that paves the way for wisdom and behavioural stability. Calmness is certainly a virtuous experience.

How can someone be calm when they are living with disturbing elements?

When we are calm from within, the chaos without can never last longer. Calmness has a greater degree of positivity that can overcome all negativity. Being calm is a feeling of being competent and compatible. We must remember that nothing can ever disturb us without our own consent. Our inner space is our exclusive possession. No one can ever infringe upon it unless welcomed. Whatever may be the situation, calm minds never give negative reactions since they are full of understanding and faith. The real meaning of the life lies in overcoming the challenges that it gives. When we are calm, we become stronger than the situation. Our inner calm can overcome all that disturbs and distracts.

What's the impact of calmness on life as a whole?

Calmness leads to strength, creativity, wisdom and truth as central to our true growth. A weak mind reacts; a strong mind resists; but a great mind always stays calm for it only knows the truth. The inner calm in every situation enhances the inner beauty too. Positive thoughts, constructive habits and creative goals together contribute to the calmness inside which greatly facilitates someone's true growth.

Mind what matters!!!

- Calmness is an essential ingredient of creativity and concentration.
- One's best self functions only when there's calmness inside.
- Calmness has a greater degree of positivity.
- Calm minds never give negative reactions since they are full of understanding and faith.
- The real meaning of life lies in overcoming the challenges that it gives.
- Calmness leads to strength, creativity, wisdom and truth.
- A weak mind reacts; a strong mind resists; but a great mind always stays calm for it only knows the truth.

THE POWER OF OUR HABITS

What's the importance of our habits?
Our habits are everything in our lives indeed! They determine our existence. A habit can influence the patterns of thinking; and, more importantly, it can transform the character. The quality of our life is largely controlled by the quality of the habits. According to Sean Covey, "Depending on what they are, our habits will either make us or break us. We become what we repeatedly do." Our habits ultimately become the instruments of our nature; and our nature is responsible for our growth as individuals. That is to say, we think and become according as the habits we develop over a period of time. In this context, Aristotle once said: "Excellence is an art won by training and habituation." In order to change our life, we need to embrace certain life-changing habits. We can never change our life in a desired manner without changing our daily routine as part of our habits. As John C. Maxwell has put it, "You'll never change your life until you change something you do daily. The secret of your success is found in your daily routine."

How can one change the bad habits?
For this, one needs to get hold of the inner strengths. The realization plays a crucial role. Our habits are usually formed around the things we like. Therefore, we should learn to dislike things that are not good for our true growth and like the ones that help us reach our goals. Moreover,

we have to control our thoughts. According to Swami Vivekananda, 'He conquers all who conquers self.' Self-control holds the key. It's only through constant practice and discipline that we can both change the bad habits and create the good ones. A positive mind always looks for explorations, whereas a negative mind looks for excuses. We need to control the mind in a positive way. Self-belief is quite instrumental in the process. We do, when we believe; and we achieve, when we do. What's more, in order to succeed, we must have the strength to overcome our own weaknesses.

What it takes to sustain a good or positive habit?

We need to remember that the most vital thing in our life is our effort; and our sincerity is what makes it effective. A conscious detachment from things, not good for our life, must be followed quite passionately. One needs to be earnest in their efforts. Purity, passion, patience and perseverance can lead someone to the realm of success and bliss. Here one story that Swami Vivekananda would tell his disciples can be mentioned. Narada was a great Yogi. He used to travel everywhere. One day Narada was passing through a forest, and saw a man who had been meditating until the white ants had built a huge mound round his body — so long had he been sitting in that position. He said to Narada, "where are you going? " Narada replied, 'I am going to heaven'. "Then ask God when He will be merciful to me; when I shall attain freedom." Further on Narada saw another man. He was jumping about, singing and dancing, and said, "Oh Narada, where are you going?" His voice and his gestures were wild. Narada said, "I am going to heaven". "Then ask when I shall be free". Narada went on.

In the course of time he came again by the same road, and there was the man who had been meditating with the ant-hill round him. He said, "Oh Narada, did you ask the Lord about me?" "Oh, Yes". "What did he say?" "The Lord told me that you would attain freedom in four more births". Then the man began to weep and wail, and said, "I have meditated until an ant-hill has grown around me, and I have four more births yet!" Narada went to the other man. "Did you ask my question?" "Oh, yes. Do you see this tamarind tree? I have to tell you that as many leaves as there are on that tree, so many times, you shall be born, and then you shall attain freedom. " The man began to dance for joy, and said, "I shall have freedom after such a short time!" A voice came, "My child, you will have freedom this minute." That was the reward of his perseverance. He was ready to work through all those births, nothing discouraged him. But the first man felt that even four more births were too long. Only perseverance like that of the man who was willing to wait eons brings about the highest result.

Is controlling the thoughts possible?

Nothing is impossible if there is a tremendous character within. According to the Bhagvad Gita, 'by renunciation and by practice can the mind be brought under control.' It's only by doing good things constantly that we can better ourselves. The will and character to continue matters. The difference between failure and success, or challenge and that of possibility, is the nature of our thoughts. Therefore, we must develop a habit of exploring our own positivity irrespective of all circumstances.

Mind what matters!!!

- Our habits shape our lives.
- In order to change our life, we need to embrace certain life-changing habits.
- Our habits are usually formed around the things we like. Therefore, we should learn to dislike things that are not good for our true growth and like the ones that help us reach our goals.
- A positive mind always looks for explorations, whereas a negative mind looks for excuses.
- In order to succeed, we must have the strength to overcome our own weaknesses.
- One needs to be earnest in their efforts.
- We must develop a habit of exploring our own positivity irrespective of all circumstances.

TECHNOLOGY AND PEACE

How's technology affecting our lives?

Observed minutely, we are gradually making our way into a subtler era of 'Intellechnology' wherein lies a reciprocal relationship between the human intellect and technology. The modern smart technologies have greater behavioural dynamics. In this context one may talk about mobile phones, various app-based communications and the underlying digital technological convergence. Today, the Communication technology has become a vibrant human necessity, quite indispensable in the usual process of life.

How is our dependency on technology?

We become dependent only when we completely surrender ourselves to something or someone, because we think we can't do anything without them. There is a difference between the affected need and the actual need. One needs to understand the difference. Why do I need it? Do I really need it or I need it just because others need it? The modern innovative communication technologies have influenced the human mind in a big way. Every mind is unique, but they seem to be affected alike by the technology.

The sustained technological intervention is leading the human mental behaviour into an uncreative realm of existence replete with the passivity, rigidity and negativity of the thoughts. In a sense, we are no more using technology these days; rather, the technology is using us owing more to our inordinate and irrational dependency. After the advent of the internet-based interactive communications including social media and new media, much of the human behaviour has been technologically determined. It has given rise to the increasing instances of techno-emotionalism.

Techno-emotionalism sounds really interesting! What is it actually?

Simply put, every technological medium has got a distinctive nature. The nature of the medium affects the nature of the communication; the nature of the communication affects the nature of our lives; and the nature of our lives affects the nature of our societies. The communication technologies can influence, control and create emotions in certain contexts. Extreme dependency on technology can be worrying. When the mind is technologically regulated or programmed, it leads to the loss of the human sensibilities. And eventually, it thinks, acts and behaves in a way bereft of human values and emotional connectivity. Therefore techno-emotionalism refers to the effects of the technological dependency on the human emotions and its behavioural consequences.

What can be the solutions in this context?

First of all, we have to work on our habits and manage ourselves. We are in a better position to understand and determine our needs as individuals. We are possessed by the technology, the moment we can't control our dependence. We must be aware of the technological determinism through effective self-management.

Secondly, we must value the genuine emotions in all our relationships. Technology must act as a facilitator, not as a controller of emotions. A value-based life believes in valuing duties towards real emotions. The virtual world of technology must under no circumstances take control over the real human world of sensitivity, receptivity and connectivity.

Thirdly, there must be efforts towards creating an ethically conscious environment for everyone we are living with and living for. We mustn't use technology irresponsibly and irrationally. This can be possible by adequate awareness, reflection and realization. Lastly, we must learn to live without negative technology as far as possible. Here, negative technology means the technology that is instrumental to the creation of the negative emotions. Every little step towards this will help. Mind must be used creatively and sensibly in the pursuit of life's goals. Moreover, we have to think about a better world for the posterity by way of self-awareness and self-management. The nature of the mind potentially influences the nature of the uses and effects of the medium. We need to remember, if we can't control the mind, the mind will surrender to the ills of the technology once and for all. Moreover, the larger benefits of any medium rest inevitably on the soundness of our minds.

Mind what matters!!!

- We become dependent only when we completely surrender ourselves to something or someone, because we think we can't do anything without them.
- In a sense, we are no more using technology these days; rather, the technology is using us owing more to our inordinate and irrational dependency.
- The nature of the medium affects the nature of the communication; the nature of the communication affects the nature of our lives; and the nature of our lives affects the nature of our societies.
- Technology must act as a facilitator, not as a controller of emotions.
- Mind must be used creatively and sensibly in the pursuit of life's goals.
- The nature of the mind potentially influences the nature of the uses and effects of the medium.

PEOPLE AND NATURES

How should we deal with people we don't like?

In the first place, we have to understand why we don't like someone. Everyone has got their own unique nature. We may not like every nature. We need to ask a question: is the person important in my life? If no, just let them be there and let's keep detached emotionally. If yes, we hardly have any option. In this case we should keep doing our duty without any expectations since our expectations would disturb the peace of the mind ultimately.

There are some people who are important, but sometimes they behave like strangers! How to deal with this situation?

It means we are emotionally attached and dependent on those people. We should never let our dignity and sense of independence perish at any cost! We must remember that we can't expect anyone to behave the way we like. If some people behave like strangers at times, it's their strange nature, not ours! Why are we worried then? Can we change their nature? If no, why are we losing our own happiness? Our happiness should be more important to us than the so-called important people with such strange natures. We should remember that if someone is genuinely connected and cares for us, they will always be there. But we can't simply expect someone to stay connected like that! Sometimes, our behaviour is affected by situations we can't control. We need to manage ourselves a lot emotionally.

Why do people change?

In fact, everything changes. It's another story that we like some changes and we don't like some. To be perfectly honest, we can't force people to love ourselves. We can't imagine our life our ways in connection with someone. The irony is that sometimes, we can't control ourselves; so, how can we think of controlling the thought-process of someone else? Whatever may be the circumstances, if there is love, it'll take care of everything. We should, therefore, trust ourselves more and stand with ourselves as boldly as possible, instead of thinking much about someone's nature and behavior. We practically have no control over that.

How to create a positive impression about ourselves?

We can't make everyone happy. This is not humanly possible. We should focus on our duties and efforts. People have different feelings in different situations. We shouldn't be affected by that. We must stay positive, strong and emotionally intelligent. Sometimes, we need to act according to the situation, have that sense of maturity to rise to the occasion. We must try to express ourselves skillfully on certain occasions. No impression is permanent. It is all situational. So, let's focus on our actions in a positive manner without bothering our head about the unwanted reactions of others. We should remember that the perception may affect the performance, but the performance can change the perception.

Mind what matters!!!

- We should keep doing our duty without any expectations since our expectations would disturb the peace of the mind ultimately.
- Whatever may be the circumstances, if there is love, it'll take care of everything.
- We can't make everyone happy. This is not humanly possible. We should focus on our duties and efforts without thinking much.
- We should remember that the perception may affect the performance, but the performance can change the perception.

POSITIVE LEADERSHIP

What is leadership?

Leadership is a process of achieving certain goals that involve leading someone to their real potential and making them realize their strengths by creating inspiring examples. Leadership is always a skill-driven and goal-oriented exercise. A leader is someone who can inspire and motivate some people towards a common goal irrespective of the inherent individual differences.

How can one become a leader?

A leader is born out of a natural will to handle responsibilities, share burdens and create a difference in whatever he or she undertakes. A good leader is always a wonderful learner. A leader learns to lead. They love to know their people and the realities they are made of. A leader is ever full of patience, passion and positivity. He or she believes in creating some great vibes around through great degrees of commitment, dedication, emotional intelligence and core involvement in the situation. A leader is never a fearmonger; rather their presence eases out fear and creates a climate of trust and confidence. We must try to reflect on the qualities of some of the great global leaders like Mahatma Gandhi, Swami Vivekananda, Nelson Mandela, Abraham Lincoln etc.

What is the biggest asset of a leader?
The biggest asset is definitely the character! If the character of a leader is positive and inspiring, he or she is perceived as a role model. Then, things become much easier. 'Trusting the leader' is very vital. But this trust can neither be commanded nor manufactured. It can only be earned by the beauty of character. A leader needs to take care of every little thing that counts. They can do so only when they work without their ego and self-interest.

What are the biggest challenges before a leader?
Working together is never an easy experience since everyone is unique as regards their perception, personality and performance. Understanding everyone's mind and emotions is what empowers a leader to a great extent. Sometimes, the leader has to make some sacrifices at personal levels and adjust to the changing situation. If a leader can't change their behaviour in the larger interest, they can never motivate people to perform on the desired scale.

The Goal Theory of Leadership!

— *A positive leader can lead both positive and negative minds, whereas a negative leader can only lead negative minds.*

— *A positive leadership creates a positive goal, whereas a negative leadership creates a negative goal which doesn't help anyone ultimately.*

— *A positive goal requires a positive behaviour in the process.*

— *The Positive Goal can be achieved only if the leadership is positive. There is no other way out!*

What are the qualities of a great leader?

Simply put, it takes courage, knowledge and message to be a great leader. We must be willing to take charge of a responsibility and try to be courageous enough to handle it towards the goal. We must know who we are working with. Knowing the strengths and weaknesses of the people and managing them accordingly is very important. More importantly, we should send our message through our performance involving an inspiring character. Moreover, we must remember that the greatest achievement of a leader is to create another leader of the same or even greater character. And this can be possible only when we, as leaders, can be able to create such inspiring characters in ourselves.

Mind what matters!!!

- If the character of a leader is positive and inspiring, he or she is perceived as a role model.
- Understanding everyone's mind and emotions is what empowers a leader to a great extent.
- If a leader can't change their behaviour in the larger interest, they can never motivate people to perform on the desired scale.
- A positive leader can lead both positive and negative minds, whereas a negative leader can only lead negative minds.
- It takes courage, knowledge and message to be a great leader.

RELATIONSHIP

What is a relationship?
A relationship can be seen as a medium of happiness. It connotes how we are related to ourselves as well as others. Relationship is not just a condition of identity or social status; rather, it has to do with love, communication, understanding, trust, acceptance, and sacrifice all the time. No relationship can ever exist without these.

What is the major barrier to a relationship?
There can be no relationship without trust. The biggest challenge to trust in any relationship is misunderstanding which results from a strong sense of self-conceit and/or ego. If you can't trust someone, you can never accept them. We must remember that mutual respect is the real basis of a relationship. Most of the problems arise due to our ego-led nature of not respecting the people's emotions.
Love and respect go together. Lack of respect also means lack of love. We must learn to be respectful to the people and their emotions in all our relationships. We should understand that the true beauty of a relationship lies in its duty, not expectations for any return.

How does a relationship affect our lives?
A beautiful life requires a beautiful relationship; and a beautiful relationship verily requires a beautiful heart. We need to have a heart that beats with love—a heart that

cares, a heart that shares and a heart that responds to both the manifest and unmanifest emotions. A true relationship creates a great emotional balance as central to the success of all our endeavours.

Understanding 'true relationship'

It suggests a relationship based on love, not anything else! There is always a clear difference between love and dependency. 'I can't live without you' doesn't necessarily mean 'I love you'! There are always two categories of people around. There are some people who need you, and there are some who love you. Those who need you may leave you anytime; but those who love you would love you even if you leave them. One can very well relate it within the practical contexts of experience. A need-based relationship has got its own limitations and challenges. It is always influenced by the nature of the needs and the related expectations. Simply put, a relationship can never be confined to the need it is based on! It has to be free from all narrowness. If a relationship is based on a need, there will be challenges whether or not the need is gratified; but, if a relationship has its origin in love and mutual acceptance, then it will continue forever, come rain or shine!

Does understanding play a key role in making a relationship successful?

Absolutely! Understanding is the lifeblood of a relationship. Understanding affects our behaviour; and our behaviour affects our relationship. So, it is how we understand each other that matters. Understanding is never that easy too. We must have a constant will, commitment and effort to understand someone. There is no such problem if you can't understand, but there is a great problem if you don't want to understand or misunderstand. And here comes the role of communication. Our communication affects our relationship a great deal. We need to communicate to create mutual understanding and acceptance. The ideal way is to both begin and complete our communication with understanding. Every small communication matters!

Understanding, therefore, is always a matter of sensitivity, receptivity and connectivity. We must have adequate patience and emotional intelligence. Understanding may cost our ego and nature, but it can save a relationship. Sometimes, very small things count. It is how we express our feelings that matters. Lastly, understanding each other is a great joy. It makes the relationship truly beautiful.

Mind what matters!!!

- No relationship can ever exist without love, communication, understanding, trust, acceptance and sacrifice.
- If you can't trust someone, you can never accept them.
- Love and respect go together. Lack of respect also means lack of love.
- Mutual respect is the real basis of a successful relationship.
- There is always a clear difference between love and dependency. 'I can't live without you' doesn't necessarily mean 'I love you'!
- Our communication affects our relationship a great deal.
- Understanding each other is a great joy. It makes the relationship truly beautiful.

DEPRESSION

What are the basic causes of depression?
Depression occurs due to various reasons. It's certainly an intense emotional phenomenon. Depression mainly results from an emotion we are extremely attached to. We need to understand that an emotion, if can't be controlled, leads to an attachment; an attachment, if can't be managed, leads to an expectation; and an expectation, if not fulfilled, leads to a lot of trouble including depression and/or things of that sort.

How can someone control the emotions?
There should be emotion in our lives. A life without emotions is hardly worth-living; but, we should be in a position to control our emotions. Emotions are enjoyable as long as they can be controlled. The problems arise when they become uncontrollable. To control or manage emotions we need to develop our capacity to know, understand and reflect on things we experience. We shouldn't make ourselves so weak that we can't live without something or someone. Our thoughts make us ultimately. We need to understand the nature of our thinking. It is how we think that affects our behaviour, and it is how we behave that affects our existence. So, our thoughts shouldn't make us weak. They must make us explore our positive strengths.

How to deal with the people around us?

Everyone in this world is unique as regards their perception, personality and performance. We need to understand this unique nature of people. When everyone is unique there can be no comparison and expectation. We simply can't expect people to behave the way we like. The less we expect externally, the more we can explore internally; and this inner exploration alone leads to excellence. The simple formula is we should stop judging, comparing with and expecting from people. Let's do our duty without judging, comparing and expecting. If someone is genuinely connected, they will act in that way. So, why worry at all?

How to make ourselves happy?

The first thing is we must love ourselves and have an unflinching self-belief in every situation. We can if we think we can. The idea of happiness is individually unique. There can be no universal formula. However, the real happiness lies within. Sometimes, it lies with smaller things and smaller goals, and sometimes it lies with the bigger ones. It all depends on our idea of happiness. We can be happy with smaller things if we can find our hearts in them. It's a matter of connecting to our real self. Happiness is indeed a choice. Nothing can ever stop us from being happy if we choose to live without expectations and negative emotions. Moreover, the real happiness leads to and comes from learning and self-exploration. It leads you to live your positivity, passion and purpose in whatever small or big spaces available. Life becomes beautiful when we replace fear with faith, pain with patience, despair with dreams, loathing with love, and ego with enlightenment. Lastly, we must realize our own uniquely precious nature and act accordingly.

Mind what matters!!!

- An emotion, if can't be controlled, leads to an attachment; an attachment, if can't be managed, leads to an expectation; and an expectation, if not fulfilled, leads to a lot of trouble.
- Emotions are enjoyable as long as they can be controlled.
- We shouldn't make ourselves so weak that we can't live without something or someone.
- We must love ourselves and have an unflinching self-belief in every situation.
- Happiness is indeed a choice. Nothing can ever stop us from being happy, if we choose to live without expectations and negative emotions.

FINDING HAPPINESS

Overcoming Loneliness

Loneliness has its own beauty. When we are alone, we are with ourselves, indeed! Our life has its various dimensions in various contexts. Amidst all the routine hustle and bustle, we hardly get time to come in contact with our deeper self that lies well within. Human life is full of challenges; but, in every challenge there is an opportunity to discover and unleash our own unique potential. We should feel the silence of our loneliness where resides the voice of the inner being. We must try to listen to it. No chain can ever limit the divinity in us; and no obstacle can ever obstruct its progress. We need to realize the divine connect in us through a spiritual approach. All the precious things are stored within us. The real happiness lies within. The inner contour of our being is incorruptible. The more we look within, the happier we become! In being alone, there is a chance of living within and growing within.

Here's RECAAP, your happiness formula

REFLECT:

A positive life is always backed by minute reflections. We need to reflect on our thoughts and behaviour in different contexts; and try to understand the need and impact of it. When we try to reflect on our behaviour as a detached spectator, we realize its essence in the entirety. Without reflection no life can ever be progressive.

EXPLORE:
Exploration is instrumental to our true growth. Everyone in this world is born unique. That way, everyone is having their unique capability as regards their perception, personality and performance. We need to explore ourselves in every situation. Exploration leads to excellence. The more we explore, the more we excel. Every situation helps us know ourselves better; and this self-knowledge leads to self-management that causes a blissful experience.

CONNECT:
We need to connect to the inner being or the better version of ourselves always. If we stay connected from within, we can't be disturbed by any circumstances of life. We need to get hold of this inner connectivity which can be achieved by the spiritual exercise of reflection and exploration.

ACCEPT and ADJUST:
Adjustment is a vital component of a progressive life. For adjustment acceptance is indispensable. We must learn the art of accepting things. If we can't perform a desired action or if we can't achieve a desired result, that isn't failure. We need to accept the experience of the effort and adjust accordingly. Sometimes, situations demand change or correction in our attitude and behaviour. We need to understand the need for wise or healthy adjustment in situations. If we are flexible enough to adjust to the changing conditions, we can truly help ourselves grow.

PRACTICE:

We need to put all our learning into constant practice. It is only through sincere practice that we can improve upon ourselves and come out with the better versions. That is to say, it is only by doing things that we can do things better. Practice brings control, and control brings perfection. Practice also makes knowledge useful. In fact, knowledge without its usefulness is as good as ignorance.

How Life should be looked at?

In the last analysis, our life is our choice and responsibility. It is only how we think about it that determines the quality of our lives. Our thinking affects our behavior; and our behaviour affects our existence. Nothing can stop our progress if we are willing to continue. We need to remember that success is a matter of effort; effort is a matter of commitment; and commitment is a matter of conviction.

Mind what matters!!!

- The more we look within, the happier we become!
- Without reflection no life can ever be progressive.
- Every situation helps us know ourselves better; and this self-knowledge leads to self-management that causes a blissful experience.
- If we stay connected from within, we can't be disturbed by any circumstances of life.
- It is only by doing things that we can do things better.
- Our thinking affects our behavior; our behaviour affects our existence.
- Success is a matter of effort; effort is a matter of commitment; and commitment is a matter of conviction.

STRESS, FITNESS & POSITIVE PERSONALITY

What's stress?

Stress is a feeling of overexertion that involves a pressure of adverse influences, circumstances etc that disturbs the natural physical, mental and emotional balance. There are so many stress factors that prevent our usual flow of work and life. There can be physical stress that occurs due to excessive physical activity and involvement. In order to get rid of the physical stress we need to have the physical skills. We should take care of our health and work on a healthy lifestyle. Regular healthy breaks from work schedules would help. Mental stress results from mental instability, lack of concentration, over-thinking and the inability to accept and enjoy the situation. Here it has to be asserted that every mind is unique and so is everyone. The mental strength has to do with learning, realization, and effective cognitive behaviour. The emotional stress occurs primarily due to an emotionally incompatible environment replete with fear, doubt, disbelief, ego, intolerance, sense of alienation and rejection.

How can fitness help?

Fitness means different things to different people. However, a standard perception of fitness defines it as an ability to respond effectively to every situation and perform to the desired result. Simply put, fitness is more about expressing one's vital potential at both the physical and mental levels. Observed minutely, the mental fitness is really crucial and central to all forms of fitness

Positive Personality: the FLOWER Theory

Fearlessness

A positive personality is centred on the positive mental fitness that involves Fearlessness, Learning, Observation, Working, Exploration and Rectification. Fearlessness is all about believing in oneself and staying motivated within. Believing is achieving. Fear as a psychological phenomenon affects all levels of fitness and creates all sorts of trouble in the process of the true growth. Self-belief is very vital in the overall development of the personality. Learning is undoubtedly the oxygen for existence. Learning causes the true growth. It can be said that 'the more we know the more we grow'. The mental fitness largely depends on the way we learn and respond to our learning. The learning attitude facilitates the inner strength and flexibility.

Constant Learning, Observation and Working

The source of learning can be anything, and all sources are equally important. One can learn from study, situations, experiences, relationships and reflections. All our actions should be driven by and lead to learning. Observation plays an important role in the process of self-improvement. When we observe our actions or behaviour we understand the cause-effect aspect to a great extent. Observation helps someone realize the core potential which is instrumental in the progressive growth of the personality. Above all, we need to work on ourselves, our weak areas.

When we work on our skills, we pave the way for self-improvement. Working on ourselves can include reading, writing, practicing, developing certain useful habits etc. For an example, for being an effective communicator we need to work on our writing skills. Writing has a greater psychological benefit. It organizes the thought process and it also creates more systematic communication behaviour. Writing also purges the negative emotions and causes a creative sublimation of the thoughts leading to a greater mental health.

Exploration and Expression

Exploration and excellence go together. The more we explore, the more we excel. One needs to explore their core creative substance. The core creative substance lies within. It is the basic spark of our personality. The core creative substance consists in our creative interests, abilities and energies. It can be explored through a process of inner exposure and experience resulting from various self-reflective exercises. Exploration should lead to expression. Expression results in creative satisfaction. Whenever we find a chance to express ourselves, we must express ourselves without any fear or hesitation.

Need for rectification

We all live in a dynamic world. Things here change every moment shaping our thoughts and actions. Therefore, we should be in a position to change and correct ourselves and adjust to the changing conditions. The faster we can rectify ourselves, the better we can perform in our fields. Human mind is a complex phenomenon, but the beauty of the mind lies in the fact that it is capable of achieving the most unachievable. Once we are mentally committed, we are unstoppable. There can be no perfection without passion. If we have passion, we have a place. When we talk of positive mental fitness, we need to emphasize purpose, passion and patience as central to all our excellence.

Understanding the Positive Mind

A positive mind never compares, never competes and never expects. It only explores, expresses, learns and celebrates. A positive mind consists in our own unique positivity that we need to explore within us. Positive mental fitness comprises positive mental strength which is of capital importance. We need to have that sense of conviction regarding our unique capability we are naturally blessed with. The mental fitness also involves the effective management of emotion and ego. Our emotion shouldn't be our essence. It shouldn't control our life. When our life is controlled by our emotion, the effort towards our goal is lost. Our own nature is responsible for both our success and failure. The nature creates character; character affects behaviour; behaviour causes experience; and experience leads to feeling. So our own nature is responsible for our feeling in every situation. Ego never lets us learn and accept things. Mental fitness is all about thinking beautifully and acting accordingly. There is no place for depression and frustration in human life since we are the sole shapers of our lives. We should remember that rejections refine us; difficulties define us and the dreams determine us!

Know the power of the mind

According to Swami Vivekananda, 'every thought is like a little hammer blow on the lump of iron which our bodies are manufacturing out of it what we want to be.' Human mind is immensely powerful. This power should be realized and channelized properly. A positive mind is the cause of a positive life. The nature of our mind greatly determines the nature of our thinking; the nature of our thinking largely affects the nature of our behaviour; and the nature of our behaviour hugely influences the nature of our being. According to Sri Aurobindo,' it is always a mistake to complain about the circumstances of our lives since they are the outward expressions of what we are ourselves'.

Knowing the inner beauty and vibes

The concept of the mental fitness essentially involves the concept of the positive mind. There should be no space for negative thoughts since they don't help anyone anyway. It should be remembered that no effort for progress ever goes in vain. Life is all about living again beyond all seasons. Nothing can disturb us without our consent. No obstacle is bigger than the effort to overcome it. No problem can ever limit its solution. No change can ever be a challenge; and no challenge can ever change the opportunity contained therein. Every difficulty comes with a new possibility. When we realize that we are unique, we grow bigger than our worries. All one needs is a positive attitude propelled by a positive mind.

Being beautiful

There is a great difference between looking beautiful and being beautiful. The former is ephemeral, whereas the latter is perpetual. The former is all about appearance; the latter has to do with actions. There should be constant efforts to explore one's inner beauty that comprises creativity, inner happiness, mental-behavioural harmony, love for life, passion for goal and patience to withstand everything. Our inner beauty exists in our vibrations that our presence carries. The positive vibrations mostly affect the levels of the mental fitness. Moreover, they help in self-realization and achieving greater levels of the consciousness. We know ourselves better than anyone else. Self-motivation holds the key. No one can motivate us except ourselves since no one except us is in a better position to know ourselves. The positive self alone causes the positive motivation within. Discovering the positive self should be the utmost priority since the positive self largely creates and sustains the positive personality.

Mind what matters!!!

- Self-belief is very vital in the overall development of the personality.
- The more we know, the more we grow.
- Exploration and excellence go together.
- Once we are mentally committed, we are unstoppable. There can be no perfection without passion.
- A positive mind never compares, never competes and never expects. It only explores, expresses, learns and celebrates.
- Our own nature is responsible for both our success and failure.
- Rejections refine us; difficulties define us and the dreams determine us!
- No obstacle is bigger than the effort to overcome it.
- Looking beautiful is ephemeral, whereas being beautiful is perpetual.

EGO AND LIFE

What are the problems the ego may lead us to?
Ego exists in one's sense of personal pride. The major problem is that the ego never lets us learn and accept things. Learning causes the true growth. In order to learn effectively one first of all needs to accept the ignorance that lies within. Ego never lets us learn and reflect on our actions or behaviour. That way, ego may lead us to an existence devoid of learning and progress.

How to manage the ego?
Ego can be managed through a process of knowledge, reflection and realization. We must develop a habit of knowing ourselves. Self-knowledge helps in self-management. Observed minutely, ego has two distinct facets. They can be called positive ego and negative ego. In any situation positive ego strives for achieving self-improvement through rigorous efforts; whereas the negative ego is replete with negative emotions including but not limited to competition, intolerance, jealousy and revenge. Ego, as commonly understood, refers to the negative ego. In order to manage ego we need to be aware of its consequences. An atmosphere of purity and positivity is a prerequisite.

Can one live without ego?
One can live surely. But, it all depends on our idea

of ego. How we understand ego is instrumental. If we can manage our ego to grow amidst all odds, there is absolutely no problem. But it shouldn't hit our goals and roles very badly. We mustn't let our ego erode our love, the essence of our life. We must remember that ego and love can never go together. So, we have to choose one. Sometimes, the ego in us bars us from being sensitive and understanding. We often find it hard to say sorry even if we commit a mistake. Love favours the relationship, while the ego favours one's personal pride and the personally perceived sense of the self which may not always work in our favour.

How to overcome the challenges posed by the ego?

We should be flexible enough to learn and accept things. Acceptance leads to expansion. We must reflect on our past actions and muse on their impact. In any case, we need to choose love over hatred, faith over fear, understanding over ignorance, sensitivity over apathy and positivity over negativity. Moreover, the vital energy of the ego can be channelized towards the efforts for growth and progress. That way, we can improve upon ourselves continually.

Mind what matters!!!

- The ego never lets us learn and accept things.
- Ego and love can never go together.
- Acceptance leads to expansion.
- Love favours the relationship, while the ego favours one's personal pride.
- In any case, we need to choose love over hatred, faith over fear, understanding over ignorance, sensitivity over apathy and positivity over negativity.

DIGITAL COMMUNICATION AND HUMAN RELATIONSHIP

Understanding the dynamics of Communication and Technology

With technology transforming life, there are momentous cultural and behavioural changes transpiring all around. The digital media and communication technologies have forced into the human life in a big way and vibrated through its subtle facets. Moreover, the digital and smart technologies have entered the core of the human emotions and created a kind of emotional determinism. Now, life has reached a sphere of experience where the reciprocal effects of the human intellect and technology are getting felt more intensely. Our lives have been largely influenced by technology leading to the rise of a new mind-style. Simply put, our mind is increasingly becoming a slave of our relationship with technology; or to be more precise, it has been reprogrammed and restructured in accordance with the dynamics of the digital relationship. Even our thoughts are considered to be useless if they lack digital flexibility or compatibility. That is to say, if we can't express our thoughts through various digital media platforms, they happen to be meaningless. That's the reason why the digital flexibility of the human mind has become a new subject of inquiry.

The changing nature of communication

Observed minutely, the nature of communication today has undergone revolutionary changes. Ever since the world has witnessed the colossal transformation in the realm of communication technologies coupled with globalization letting the market forces rule supreme, there has been a mega metamorphosis in every walk of human life. Propelled swiftly by digitalization, the behavioural dimensions of life are being affected by the technological innovations every moment. Every medium has got its own unique nature. The nature of a particular medium affects the nature of our communication; the nature of our communication affects the nature of our lives; and the nature of our lives affect the nature of our societies. This is how the technology operates psychologically and affects our social existence. To quote the Canadian philosopher and media theorist Marshal McLuhan, 'we shape our tools, and thereafter our tools shape us'.

Technology and purpose

Today, when we look at our own digital worlds, we may feel the low levels of human sensibility specifying the concepts of the human relationship. We often love to lose ourselves in our smart-tech worlds and forget our real purposes. We have no idea when a relationship gets deleted from our life as we try to display it. We keep so engrossed technologically that we can't find time for ourselves. We are never aware of the erosion of our true being in pursuance of some mirage-like pleasure in the realm of our psycho-technological existence. Our personality is composed of various physical, mental and emotional characteristics. We need to keep in mind that beyond the virtual life there is a real world existing where we have forgotten the real reason and purpose of our existence.

Conflict and Compulsion

These days, we hardly find time to talk to our parents, teachers and people who are instrumental to our overall making. If we ever want to wish someone on some occasion, we think that a text message with an emoji or GIF is more than enough. If we want to invite someone, the same digital stuff will do. But, can these things ever generate the same intimate feelings? Can the technological flexibility ever sustain the core of our relationships? It's time we should realize that our technological innovations shouldn't kill our ethical values and sense of being human.

Need for understanding

The beauty of our life lies largely in the beauty of our relationships. In order to make our relationships beautiful we need to respect them. And we can do so if only we have love and sensitivity inside. Our virtual world gradually makes us something that can never be ourselves. A beautiful relationship is possible only on the basis of acceptance, trust, understanding, sacrifice and love. It is never possible by any other means. Today, we definitely share so many things with so many people over the digital media, but we hardly care. This is the basic cause of all unpleasant experiences. We need to understand that our relationship is the real medium of our life; and we alone are responsible for our relationships. A relationship needs more human caring, not digital sharing! More importantly, the beauty of a relationship lies in its duty which the digital technology is simply incapable of.

Mind what matters!!!

- Every medium has got its own unique nature.
- Our technological innovations shouldn't kill our ethical values and sense of being human.
- The beauty of our life lies largely in the beauty of our relationships.
- The beauty of a relationship lies in its duty which the digital technology is simply incapable of.
- A relationship needs more human caring, not technological sharing!

SELF-MANAGEMENT AND MOTIVATION

What is management?

Management can be understood as a process based on three major elements—skills, resources and goals. The process certainly involves the skillful handling of resources to achieve certain goals. For effective management, one needs to have a greater understanding of the skills, resources and the goals in specific contexts. This understanding will lead to setting appropriate goals; working on the required sets of skills; and getting the most suitable resources. As a continuous process management is more about learning, reflection and adjustment.

What is self-management?

Self-management is a process of knowing one's strengths and weaknesses; and working on them in the positive direction of self-improvement leading to the fulfillment of some greater goals. This is central to the development of a positive personality and achieving efficiency in life's key areas. It all begins with understanding the nature of thoughts. Our thinking determines our behaviour and our behaviour determines our existence. The nature of our thoughts influences the nature of our character. Thoughts result into traits and traits lead to tendencies. In the words of Swami Vivekananda, thoughts are the foundation of our being and 'we are what our thoughts have made us; so take care about what you think. Words are secondary. Thoughts live; they travel far.'

How can one do self-management?
One can do it through self-awareness, self-belief and self-motivation. We must be aware of our goals and then we need to know our strengths that will facilitate and the weaknesses that will hinder our progress. It is only through our own positivity that we can overcome our own negativity. As Swamiji has put it, 'All power is within you. You can do anything and everything. Believe in that. Don't believe that you are weak...Stand up and express the divinity within you.' We need to understand that none can motivate us but ourselves. There must be greater levels of self-awareness. The more we are aware, the better we can manage. This is a constant process. It requires purpose, patience, passion and positive perseverance. We must concentrate on our positive aspects, our strengths; and create powerfully positive vibrations to help them grow further. This will lead to self-improvement. Positive concentration will lead to positive response all the time.

What's the role of self-motivation in the process?
Self-motivation is very crucial. It keeps you focused and goal-conscious. Self-belief is instrumental to self-motivation. We need to believe in ourselves, our inner strengths. We can if we think we can. Believing is fundamental to achieving. There may be limitations and challenges present in different forms. Yet, our inner-belief and motivation to move forward must continue against all adversities. Self-motivation creates a positive consciousness

that creates a positive character leading to positive thinking and behaviour. It's a matter of creating positive energies through our thoughts and actions. Positive thoughts give us strength, whereas the negative thoughts make us weak from within. Self-motivation helps us in finding the sources of the positive energies. Energies matter! And when we stay motivated, we can lock the negative sources and unlock the positive ones. Our life certainly lies in our strengths—in our positive actions, not in our weaknesses. Self-motivation keeps us alive!

Mind what matters!!!

- The process of management certainly involves the skillful handling of resources to achieve certain goals.
- Self-management is a process of knowing one's strengths and weaknesses; and working on them in the positive direction of self-improvement leading to the fulfillment of some greater goals.
- The nature of our thoughts influences the nature of our character.
- Believing is fundamental to achieving.
- Positive thoughts give us strength, whereas the negative thoughts make us weak from within.
- Our life certainly lies in our strengths!
- Self-motivation helps us in finding the sources of the positive energies.

IMPORTANCE OF MOTHER LANGUAGE

What's the importance of mother language in our lives?

A mother language is important in the sense that it builds the primary structures of the cognitive and communication behaviour. Mother language is the language of the consciousness. It enriches our creativity and enhances our thought patterns. It's a great instrument for learning. When we learn something in our mother tongue, we understand it better since the contextual decoding is done more effortlessly in the mother tongue than in any other languages. One's mother tongue is central to their overall intellectual understanding and creative growth.

How does the mother tongue affect our lives?

According to Nelson Mandela, 'if you talk to a man in a language he understands, that goes to his head. If you talk to him in his language, that goes to his heart'. Such is the observation of a leader! The mother language is more sensitive, receptive and connective in nature. The mother tongue influences the process of encoding a great deal. It helps us in comprehending, identifying and relating to symbols we learn, understand and use in our everyday communications.

The mother tongue is full of the creative rhythm, purity and cognitive flexibility. Poet Kim Hyesoon once mentioned: 'the rhythm of my body is the same as my mother tongue. It is in this rhythm where I find sanctity, that I can return to my mother who's everywhere in the universe!'

How does the mother tongue affect our learning?

Yes, the mother tongue plays a key role in all our learning. In fact it's an effective instrument for effective learning. The mother tongue brings in a greater degree of interest, emotion and an enhanced memory in the process that makes the learning more useful and fulfilling in the related contexts. The more we learn, the more we think; and the more we think, the more we express. With the mother tongue this psychological process becomes more fruitful and rewarding. According to a famous communication theorist Marshall McLuhan, our mother tongue shapes our perceptions for life. Also Brigham Young once said: 'see that your children are properly educated in the rudiments of their mother tongue, and then let them proceed to higher branches of learning.'

How does the mother language influence our linguistic abilities?

It does affect in a big way! If we aren't properly exposed to our mother tongue, we'll definitely miss out on the patterns of effective learning and its pragmatic values. The mother tongue alone can make our learning more meaningful by creating more possibilities of reflections and knowledge without any cognitive conflicts. According to Mahatma Gandhi, 'if some people are ignorant of the mother tongue, linguistic starvation will abide'. Swami Vivekananda also emphasized on the role of the mother tongue in shaping our cognitive, intellectual and spiritual experiences. According to him, 'the mother tongue is to the mind as blood is to the body. Mother tongue is the best medium for learning and transmitting information, ideas and knowledge'. He accentuated the very words that everyman is capable of receiving knowledge if it is imparted in his own language. Therefore, we must develop a habit of reading and writing something daily in the mother tongue in the larger interests of our life, culture and society.

Mind what matters!!!

- Mother language is the language of the consciousness. It enriches our creativity and enhances our thought patterns.
- The mother tongue brings in a greater degree of interest, emotion and an enhanced memory in the process that makes the learning more useful and fulfilling in the related contexts.
- The more we learn, the more we think; and the more we think, the more we express.
- If we aren't properly exposed to our mother tongue, we'll definitely miss out on the patterns of effective learning and its pragmatic values.
- One's mother tongue is central to their overall intellectual understanding and creative growth.

PUBLIC RELATIONS

What is Public Relations?

Public Relations involves a strategic process of relationship-building based on communication, understanding, trust and acceptance. It also involves elements like positive intention and responsible behaviour. Positive intention is central to earning public trust. We can't accept something as long as we don't trust them. Trust leads to acceptance; acceptance leads to relationship; and relationship facilitates persuasion which is the ultimate goal of any public relations activity.

Role of communication in Public Relations

Communication is the lifeblood of PR. In fact, it's more of a total communication strategy. Communication in PR is of a two-dimensional character: communicating with understanding and communicating for understanding. Here the communicator first understands the public behaviour through adequate research and then designs the communication effectively for the understanding of the public. Communication acts as the foundation for any relationship. Communication causes understanding; understanding creates trust; trust leads to acceptance; and acceptance fosters relationships. Therefore, the nature of the communication can determine the nature of the relationship and vice-versa!

Ideal process of Public Relations

Any PR activity must start with research: research

about the public, their behavioural dimensions etc. Research leads to understanding and better management of the communication process. Edward Bernays, in an interview in 1991, said, "PR today is horrible. Any dope, any nitwit, any idiot can call himself or herself a Public Relations Practitioner." He regarded PR as a social science.

Research leads to understanding. Understanding the public behaviour helps in the selection of appropriate tool or medium for communication. Once the medium is selected, the specific content can be created; since the content is always medium sensitive. The next step is communication with the goal of public understanding. Here, the public must understand your communication and, more importantly, your positive intention. And then evaluation of the public attitude determines the communication effectiveness. Now the acronym can be RUMCCUE: Research, Understanding, Medium, Content, Communication, Understanding and Evaluation.

Major goals of Public Relations

Ivy Lee, often considered to be the founder of the modern Public Relations, in his 'Declaration of Principles' published in 1905, states that the public should receive 'prompt and accurate information concerning subjects which it is of value and interest to the public to know about,' concerning businesses and public institutions.

Edward Bernays (2013), another founding figure, wrote: "The three main elements of PR are practically as old as society: informing people, persuading people or integrating people with people. Of course, the means and methods of accomplishing these ends have changed as society has changed." Public Relations works on the level of public consciousness. Here, information is important, but intention is even more important. It has to do with decency, dedication and discipline a great deal!

Skills in Public Relations

There can be four broader sets of skills: Communication skills, Behavioural skills, Research skills and Situational skills. The communication skills may comprise good command over language, appropriate body language, technological orientation, decent communication temperament and contextual understanding. The behavioural skills may include managing one's ego, emotions and patience.

Moreover, it also calls for a greater degree of emotional intelligence and self-reflection. Research skills may include the knack and knowledge of research, analysis, innovation and creativity. Situational skills are also very important. Sometimes we need to act as per the situational demands which may require the abilities to respond with the presence of mind, experience, commonsense, and situational wisdom.

Mind what matters!!!

- Positive intention is central to earning public trust. We can't accept something as long as we don't trust them.
- Communication acts as the foundation for any relationship.
- Communication causes understanding; understanding creates trust; trust leads to acceptance; and acceptance fosters relationships.
- Information is important, but intention is even more important.
- Public Relations involves a strategic process of relationship-building based on communication, understanding, trust and acceptance.

Black Eagle Books

www.blackeaglebooks.org
info@blackeaglebooks.org

Black Eagle Books, an independent publisher, was founded as a nonprofit organization in April, 2019. It is our mission to connect and engage the Indian diaspora and the world at large with the best of works of world literature published on a collaborative platform, with special emphasis on foregrounding Contemporary Classics and New Writing.

www.ingramcontent.com/pod-product-compliance
Lightning Source LLC
Chambersburg PA
CBHW021627080526
44585CB00013BA/905